Published by Constance Omawumi Kola-Lawal
© 2014
ISBN 978-1-909204-33-1

Several sources of information have been consulted in the compilation of this book. The author/publisher cannot verify the absolute accuracy of all information.

All rights reserved. No part of this publication may be reproduced in any form or by any means (electronic, photocopying, recording or otherwise) without the prior written permission of the publisher. Any person infringing these rights will be liable to prosecution and civil claims.

About the author

"I've always thought that national identity is inextricably linked with how we see ourselves in the world".

Constance Omawumi Kola-Lawal

Constance is a health, safety and environment professional who is passionate about disseminating knowledge. She has BSc and MSc degrees in Pharmacology and Environmental Technology from the University of Lagos and Imperial College, London. She is awaiting a PhD degree in Environmental Management from the University of Salford, Manchester, England.

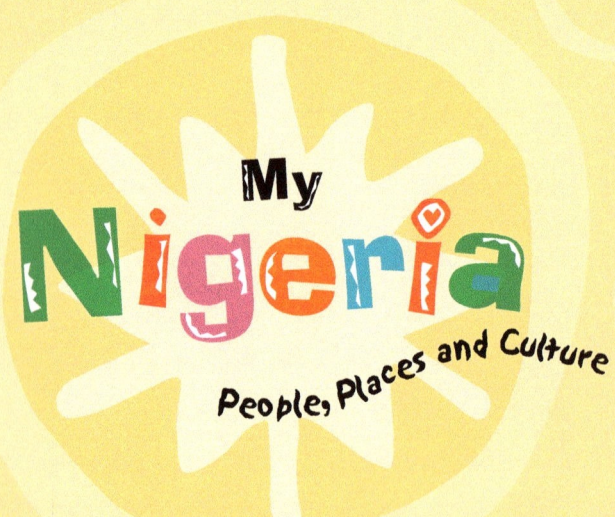

Contents

Page 1
Welcome to Nigeria
An introduction to a beautiful and diverse country, showing the Map of Nigeria with all the States, and some interesting facts and figures about Nigeria.

Page 5
The People of Nigeria
Meet 15 tribes of Nigeria, as well as some Nigerian traditional rulers.

Page 37
The Foods of Nigeria
Learn about delicious Nigerian foods and snacks.

Page 61
Places in Nigeria
From palaces to national parks - learn about some of the wonderful places in Nigeria.

Page 74
Nigerian Life
Have fun finding out about Nigerian festivals, dancers, instruments and games!

Page 90
Nigerian Pride
The Nigerian Pledge, the Nigerian Anthem and the Nigerian flag.

Welcome to Nigeria!

Hi - my name is Tishe. I am 9 years old, and I live in Lagos, Nigeria with my family. Last holidays, my family and I went on a tour of our beautiful country. Did you know it is the most populous country in Africa - with a population of nearly 170 million? We met many of the different peoples of Nigeria, and tasted lots of delicious foods! We visited interesting towns and cities, went to some festivals, and saw some wonderful dancers. We even learnt how to play some new games! We visited amazing places like the Emir's Palace and the National Arts Theatre. At the National Parks we saw lots of animals - elephants, lions and gorillas! We even climbed to the top of Zuma Rock! On the following pages you will see pictures and learn some interesting facts from our travels through Nigeria. Please enjoy and share our trip around Nigeria!

Tishe
:)

Today I ate Akara and Ogi for the first time - it was delicious!

We climbed up Zuma rock!

Welcome to Nigeria

Map of Nigeria

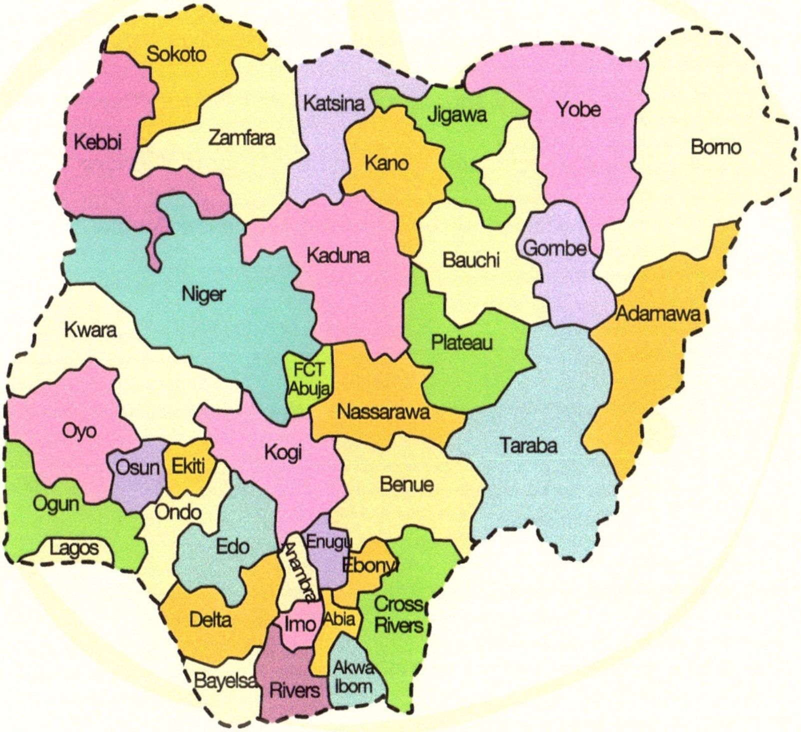

Welcome to Nigeria

Facts about Nigeria

Nigeria is one of the largest countries in Africa, and has many diverse cultures and peoples. Nigeria is made up of 36 states and a Federal Capital Territory. The name 'Nigeria' comes from the River Niger which runs through the country. Nigeria's neighbours are Benin Republic in the West, Chad and Cameroun in the East and Niger in the North. Nigeria is bordered by the Atlantic Ocean in the South.

Capital city of Nigeria: Abuja (Federal Capital Territory)

Largest lake: Lake Chad - located at the junction of Nigeria, Niger, Chad, and Cameroun

Largest River: River Niger

National flower: Costus spectabilis

Languages: English (official), Hausa, Yoruba, Igbo and more than 200 others

Currency: Naira and kobo

National bird of Nigeria: Black crowned Crane

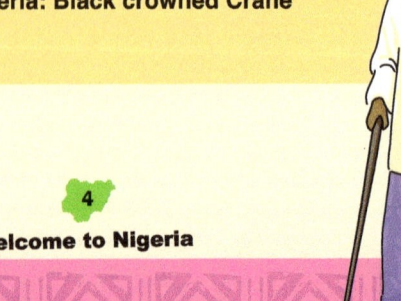

Welcome to Nigeria

The People of Nigeria

Yoruba, Fulani, Calabar, fisherman, footballers, Emir's and Sultans – come and meet them all

A Yoruba man

The Yoruba tribe originate from the age old Ile-Ife kingdom. Today they occupy the South Western states of Nigeria- Lagos, Oyn, Ogun Ondo, Osun and Ekiti states. They are often called the 'merry making' tribe of Nigeria!

The People of Nigeria

A Hausa woman

The Hausa tribe come from the Northern part of Nigeria. They are great farmers, herdsmen and traders. They speak the native Hausa language.

An Igbo man

The Igbos are a large ethnic group from South Eastern Nigeria. Rural Igbos are mostly craftsmen, traders and farmers.

The People of Nigeria

An Ijaw woman

The Ijaw tribe can be found in the Niger Delta region of Nigeria. Rural Ijaw are mostly migrant fishermen.

An Efik man

The Efik of Cross Rivers are closely related to the Ibibio of Akwa Ibom state. Traditional Efik are fishermen and traders.

The People of Nigeria

A Calabar woman

People from Calabar can be found mainly in the Cross Rivers state in Nigeria. They speak the Efik language and their king is known as the 'Obong of Calabar'.

The People of Nigeria

An Urhobo man

The Urhobo are a coastal community tribe originating from the Niger Delta Region of Nigeria. Much of Urhobo culture is influenced by their closeness to rivers, lakes and the sea.

The People of Nigeria

A Tiv man

The Tiv come from Benue state in Nigeria. Traditionally they wear a striking black and white stiped material. The Tiv are great farmers.

14

The People of Nigeria

An Ibibio man

The Ibibio mainly come from Akwa Ibom state in Southern Nigeria. As they live near the coast, they are good fishermen.

The People of Nigeria

A Fulani woman

The Fulani people are found in Northern Nigeria and many other countries in West, Central and North Africa. They are primarily herdsmen.

The People of Nigeria

An Itsekiri woman

Most Itsekiris are found in Warri City, Delta State and also in Edo and Ondo states. The Kingdom of Warri is ruled by a traditional ruler called the Olu of Warri.

The People of Nigeria

A Nupe man

The Nupe can be found mostly in Niger and Kwara states of Nigeria. They are known for their beautiful wood carvings.

The People of Nigeria

An Idoma man

The Idoma people live in Benue state in Nigeria. Traditional Idoma are great hunters and warriors.

The People of Nigeria

A Benin woman

The Benin people are a great people from Edo state in Nigeria. They are ruled by the 'Oba of Benin'. The ancient Benin people had a strong artistic culture, making sculptures of ivory, iron and bronze.

The People of Nigeria

A Kanuri woman

The Kanuri can be found mainly in Borno State of Nigeria. They have a traditional ruler called the 'Emir of Borno'.

The People of Nigeria

A Nigerian market woman

Market women and men sell food, clothes and provisions in many large and small markets in Nigeria.

The People of Nigeria

A Nigerian cattle rearer

Cattle rearers come from the northern part of Nigeria. They move all over the country, looking for food and water for their cattle.

The People of Nigeria

A Nigerian fisherman

Nigerians love fish! Fishermen use canoes and fishing nets to catch large and small fish.

The People of Nigeria

A Nigerian youth corper

A youth corper is a university or polytechnic graduate who helps the development of Nigeria. He/she does this by working and providing community service in a Nigerian city for one year.

The People of Nigeria

A Nigerian policeman

The Nigeria Police Force started in 1861 with just 30 men. The duty of the Nigeria Police Force is to provide a safe environment for everyone living in Nigeria.

The People of Nigeria

A Nigerian traffic warden

Nigerian traffic wardens are fondly called 'yellow fever' because they wear a bright orange shirt. They help to keep order on Nigerian roads.

The People of Nigeria

A Nigerian footballer

The Nigerian football team is called the Super Eagles. The Super Eagles have done Nigeria proud by appearing in the World Cup several times and winning many football trophies.

Nigerian Traditional Rulers

30
The People of Nigeria

A Nigerian Benin Oba

The Oba of Benin, or Omo N'Oba, is the traditional leader of the Edo People.

The People of Nigeria

A Nigerian Sultan

The Sultan is a traditional leader who rules the Fulani and Hausa in Northern Nigeria.

The People of Nigeria

A Nigerian Alaafin

In the Yoruba language, the word Oba means king or ruler. In Oyo the Oba is referred to as the Alaafin.

The People of Nigeria

A Nigerian Emir

The Emir of Kano comes from the Northern Nigeria - the state of Kano.

34
The People of Nigeria

A Nigerian Obi

Obi is a name used for a king in Igboland in Nigeria. He is highly respected and represents the people in all their affairs.

35

The People of Nigeria

A Nigerian Oba

The word Oba means king in Yoruba language. Really all kings in Yorubaland can be called Oba!!

A Nigerian Obong

The Obong is a political and spiritual head of the Ibibio people.

The People of Nigeria

A Nigerian Ooni

The Ooni of Ile-Ife is the ruler of the ancient Ile-Ife kingdom in Yorubaland. This title is many centuries old.

The People of Nigeria

PRIDE OF NIGERIA

dodo, chin chin, moi moi, puff puff, coconut candy and lots more!!!

The Foods of Nigeria

The Foods of Nigeria

Jollof rice and chicken

This is a Nigerian favourite! Rice is cooked in tomatoes, peppers, oil and spices. Jollof rice is delicious with chicken.

The Foods of Nigeria

Beans and dodo

In Nigeria beans is eaten in various forms - boiled or stewed with tomatoes, peppers and spices. It is often eaten with fried plantain (dodo), grated cassava (gari) or bread.

The Foods of Nigeria

Moi Moi

Moi Moi is a rich steamed beans cake which is eaten all over Nigeria and beyond. It is often served with ogi or custard, and can be eaten with jolloff rice or on its own.

The Foods of Nigeria

Akara and ogi

Akara are fritters made from black eyed beans that have been ground, mixed with onions and spices and then deep fried. It is delicious when eaten with ogi or custard.

The Foods of Nigeria

Tuwo shinkafa

Tuwo shinkafa is a northern Nigerian dish. It is a thick rice pudding, shaped into balls and usually eaten with soup or stew.

The Foods of Nigeria

Edikaikong

Edikaikong is a very nutritious soup made from a variety of leafy green vegetables, with chicken, meat or fish. It is a traditional dish of the Efik and Calabar people, but is also eaten all over Nigeria.

Efo Riro

Efo Riro is a rich and nutritious vegetable soup from Yorubaland. It is cooked with green, leafy vegetables and a variety of meats such as beef, goat meat, shaki (tripe), cow's foot, chicken and seafood.

The Foods of Nigeria

Amala with gbegiri and ewedu

Gbegiri soup is usually served with amala, ewedu (made from boiling crushed vegetables) and red stew. Gbegiri is made from ground beans, onions, palm oil and spices.

The Foods of Nigeria

Pounded yam and egusi soup

Yam tubers are boiled and pounded into a smooth, fluffy paste. Pounded yam can be eaten with many sauces including egusi soup, which is made with egusi (melon) seeds.

The Foods of Nigeria

Eba and okro soup

Eba is made by cooking grated cassava (gari) into a rough paste. It is also eaten with several soups including okro soup, which is made by cooking okros in oil, tomatoes, peppers and spices.

The Foods of Nigeria

Yam pottage

Cubes of yam are cooked in palm oil, tomatoes, peppers and spices. Yam pottage has a lovely orange color.

Banga soup and starch

Starch is made by cooking raw starch with a little palm oil to give a yellow translucent paste. Starch can be eaten with many soups including palm nut (banga) soup.

Goat meat pepper soup

Pepper soup is a favourite Nigerian food where all kinds of meat are cooked in a blend of special spices and pepper.

The Foods of Nigeria

Nigerian Snacks

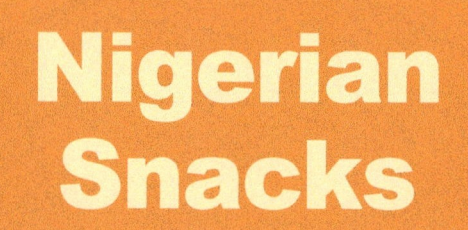

The Foods of Nigeria

Roasted corn and coconut

Corn cobs are roasted over hot charcoals and can be eaten with fresh coconut or local pears.

Puff Puff and buns

These are favourite Nigerian snacks made out of wheat flour and yeast. The flour paste is deep fried into balls.

Chin Chin

Chin chin is a popular snack made by deep frying small blocks of wheat flour paste.

Plantain chips

These are sliced and fried strips of ripe or unripe plantain. The chips are spiced with salt, pepper or sugar.

Dodo ikire

This spicy snack is made from over ripe plantain spiced with pepper.

Suya

Spicy and hot suya is made by grilling thinly sliced meat over an open flame. The meat is heavily spiced with pepper, ginger and special spices.

The Foods of Nigeria

Boli and roasted ground nuts

Boli is roasted plantain. It is delicious with groundnuts.

The Foods of Nigeria

Kokoro

Kokoro is a sweet, fried snack made from maize flour, cassava and sugar.

The Foods of Nigeria

Gurudi and coconut candy

Gurudi and coconut candy are sweets crisp snacks made from coconut.

The Foods of Nigeria

beaches, palaces, waterfalls, theatres, National Parks, gorillas, lions, elephants!

Places in Nigeria

Places in Nigeria

Lekki Peninsula

Lekki is a peninsula east of Victoria Island in Lagos, Nigeria. It is a busy coastal area with sandy beaches, shops, restaurants and residential homes. There is much commercial development and it is a gateway to southwest Nigeria via the Epe Bridge and the Lagos expressway.

Places in Nigeria

Olumo Rock

An age-old rock in Abeokuta, Ogun State in western Nigeria, Olumo Rock is a popular tourist destination. The name 'Abeokuta' stands for 'beneath the rock' in Yoruba language.

Places in Nigeria

The National Arts Theatre

The National Arts Theatre was built as an icon of the rich culture of arts in Nigeria. This magnificent building is shaped like an army general's cap!

Places in Nigeria

Gurara Falls

The Gurara waterfalls are a beautiful sight in Niger State in central Nigeria. It is potentially a tourists delight and is perfect for swimming in the dry season.

Obudu Cattle Ranch

This beautiful cattle ranch is in Cross Rivers State in southern Nigeria. It is set in a mountainous area with low hanging clouds. In some places in Obudu, your head can actually touch the clouds!

Zuma Rock

Zuma Rock is a large monolith located
in north central Nigeria.
It is immediatly North of Nigeria's capital Abuja,
and stands 725 meters above its surrounds. Zuma Rock
is sometimes referred to as the 'Gateway to Abuja'.
It is also depicted on the 100 Naira note.

Places in Nigeria

An Emir's palace

Emirs palaces are beautiful buildings decorated with colourful brick and metalwork. The palace guards wear brightly coloured turbans and dashikis.

Places in Nigeria

An Oba's palace

Obas palaces are decorated with interesting carvings around the buildings walls. Carvings are made from bronze, brass, stone, ceramic or ivory, depending on where the Oba originates from.

Places in Nigeria

A Sultan's palace

Sultans palaces are magnificently decorated buildings with intricately carved and gilded interiors.

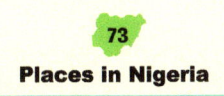

Places in Nigeria

An Obi's palace

Obis live in simple buildings guarded by palace guards. The guards carry wide swords painted in gold.

Places in Nigeria

A Nigerian market place

Nigerian markets are colourful meeting points of all cultures of the country. Fresh foods, provisions, cloths, cosmetics, electronics and much more are sold in the markets.

Places in Nigeria

National parks of Nigeria

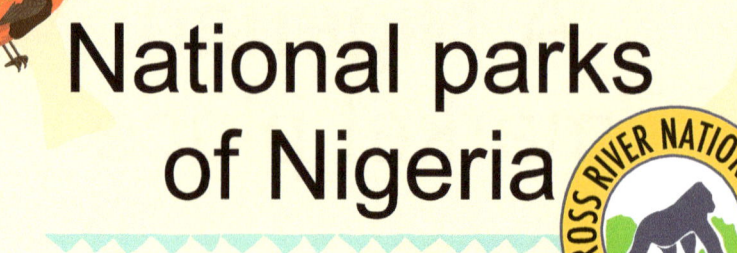

Nigeria has many national parks with a large variety of wildlife. Elephants, hyenas, gorillas and giraffes can all be found here!

National Parks in Nigeria: Kainji, Chad Basin National Park, Cross Rivers, Kamuku, Old Oyo, Gashaka Gumti, Yankari

Places in Nigeria

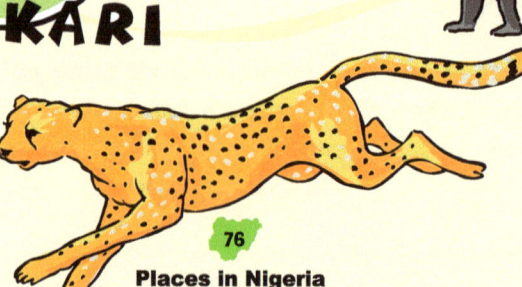

PRIDE
OF
NIGERIA

festivals, dancers, games, musical instruments

Nigerian Life

78
Nigerian Life

Nigerian Festivals

The Argungu Festival

This important fishing festival has been held since 1934 by fishermen in Kebbi State, Nigeria.
It lasts for 4 days.

Nigerian Life

Nigerian Festivals

The Durbar Festival

The Durbar is held in many cities in northern Nigeria. During the festival, brightly dressed riders and horses parade with the Emir to and from his palace. It is very colourful!

Nigerian Festivals

The Eyo Festival

This is a Yoruba cultural festival held in Lagos State, Nigeria. The festival masquerades are dressed in white, parading to the Oba's palace. The Eyo festival is over 150 years old.

Nigerian Life

Nigerian Dancers

Yoruba Dancers

The music-loving Yoruba tribe has several interesting dances and dance troupes. Dancers usually wear traditional aso-oke material.

Nigerian Life

Nigerian Dancers

Benue Dancers

Dressed in black and white stripes, they are dancers from the north central Benue State.

Nigerian Life

Nigerian Dancers

Hausa Dancers

Hausa dancers from the north eastern and western parts of Nigeria usually dance to wind instruments.

Nigerian Life

Nigerian Dancers

Igbo Dancers

There are many exciting dances from all over Igboland. Igbo dancing is very physical and energetic.

Nigerian Life

Nigerian Games

Ayo

Ayo is the Yoruba word for a game played with a locally carved wooden board and seed pebbles. The player that collects the most pebbles is the winner!

Nigerian Life

Nigerian Games

Suwe

Suwe is played by hopping on square sections drawn on the ground. It is much like the popular game hopscotch. The player throws a stone into a square, and has to hop to the end of the squares without stepping in the one with the stone.

Nigerian Life

Nigerian Games

Ten Ten

Ten ten is an old traditional game usually played by girls. Two girls stand opposite each other, clapping their hands and hop-stepping. The winner is the girl who places her foot forward first at the end of each round.

Nigerian Musical Instruments

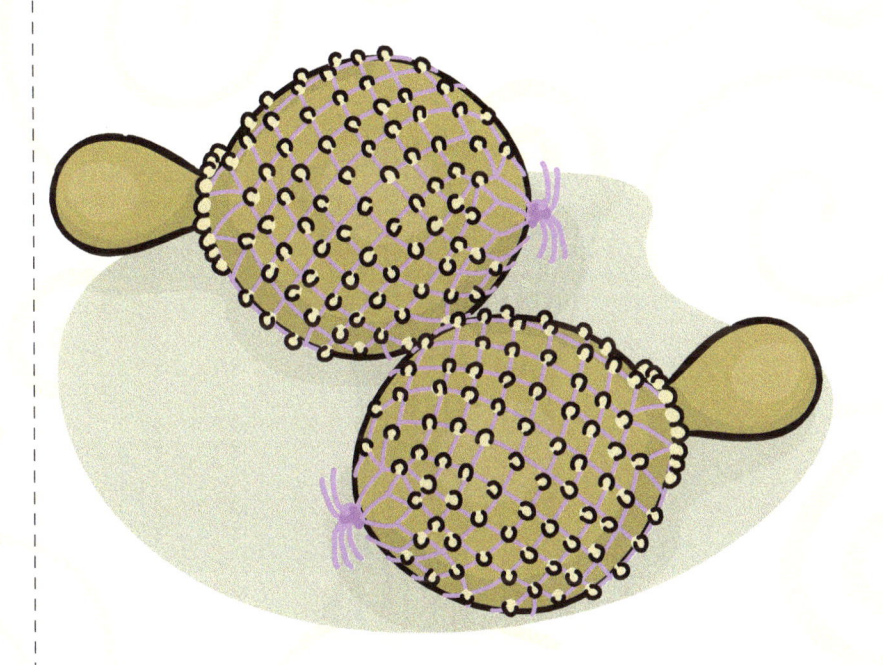

Shekere

Shekere is the Nigerian name for a popular African musical instrument. It is made by weaving seeds or beads into a rope net and attaching it to a hollow gourd. It makes a lovely sound!

Nigerian Life

Nigerian Musical Instruments

The Drum

The drum is one of the most significant musical instruments in Nigeria. Nearly all tribes in Nigeria dance to the wonderful and lively beat of the drum.

Nigerian Musical Instruments

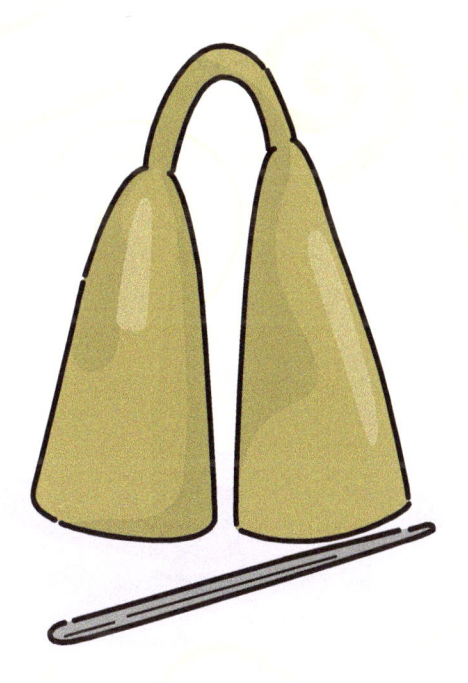

Gong

Gongs in Nigeria are made of metal or rock. They are hit with a stick to make a loud sound.

Nigerian Musical Instruments

Ivory Horn

This is a special horn made out of ivory or animal horn. When blown, it makes a loud piercing sound.

Nigerian Life

Nigerian Musical Instruments

Armpit talking drum

When played under the armpit, the armpit talking drum can be used to imitate the human voice.

Nigerian Life

Nigerian money

Naira and kobo

94
Nigerian Life

**PRIDE
OF
NIGERIA**

Nigerian Pride

The Nigerian Pledge

I pledge to Nigeria my country,

To be faithful, loyal and honest,

To serve Nigeria with all my strength,

To defend her unity,

And uphold her honour and glory,

So help me God.

The Nigerian National Anthem

"Arise, O Compatriots"

Arise, O compatriots,

Nigeria's call obey

To serve our Fatherland

With love and strength and faith.

The labor of our heroes past

Shall never be in vain,

To serve with heart and might

One nation bound in freedom, peace and unity

O God of creation

Direct our noble cause

Guide our leaders right

Help our youth the truth to know

In love and honesty to grow

And living just and true

Great lofty heights attain

To build a nation where peace

And justice shall reign

Thanks for joining me on my journey.
Hope you enjoyed learning about Nigeria
as much as I did.

We are all proudly Nigerian!

Tishe ☺

Nigerian Pride

**Also by
Constance Omawumi Kola-Lawal**

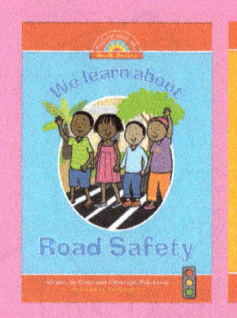

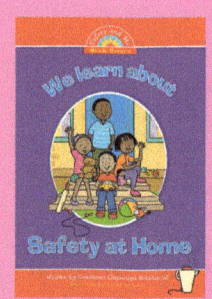

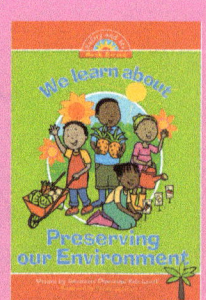

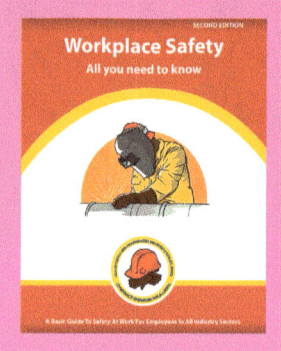

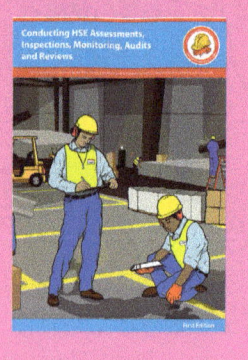

Lightning Source UK Ltd.
Milton Keynes UK
UKHW020448280921
391283UK00006B/188